LESSONS FOR THE
HEART

ROBERT L SCARBROUGH

WestBow
PRESS
A DIVISION OF THOMAS NELSON

WestBow Press books may be ordered through booksellers or by contacting:

WestBow Press
A Division of Thomas Nelson
1663 Liberty Drive
Bloomington, IN 47403
www.westbowpress.com
1-(866) 928-1240

ISBN: 978-1-4497-1915-9 (sc)

Library of Congress Control Number: 2011930944

Printed in the United States of America

WestBow Press rev. date: 06/03/2011

CONTENTS

Witchcraft 1

Demons 5

Hell 9

Death 13

Heaven 15

Money 19

Charity 23

Greed 25

Did Jesus Christ Sin? 27

Is Jesus Christ the Only Way? 29

Is Jesus Really Coming Soon? 33

Forgiveness 37

Compassion 39

Love 41

Israel 45

Muslims 49

War 51

Bondage 55

Humility 57

Peace 59

Pride 61

Salvation 63

Creation 67

Abortion 71

Family 75

Family Values 77

Wife/Husband 79

Homosexuality 83

Stress 85

Laziness 87

Prophecy 89

Adultery 93

Adversity 95

WITCHCRAFT

This is a subject that nowadays not too many people want to believe in. There is a big debate out there that you have good and bad witchcraft. I am here to tell you that it is not true. There is no such thing as good witchcraft. It's a wolf with sheep's clothing. I know this because I once got involved in it. I wanted power and it gave me more then I asked for. I had no idea what I was in store for. My world was forever changed when I walked into that lifestyle. It all started when I was about fourteen and I started following the wrong people. The first one I met led me into rebellion, smoking, cussing, not to mention gaining a lot of my trust. Then the second person I met was the one who led me into my spiritual downfall. Within a matter of twenty months, I went from singing praises of God to praising anything to do with Satan. I would listen to all kinds of hard rock and the one I loved the most was Marilyn Manson. For the ones out there that do not know who he is, he is what some would call a shock rocker. Some believe what he does is just entertainment but I can tell you from firsthand experience that it is much more than you know. Over the months that I carried on this lifestyle, I got further and further into the dark side. I had a major thing for vampires and would frequently watch just about anything to do with them. I began to get a whole new look, attitude, and started to lose touch with reality. By the time I was half way through my fifteenth year, I began to feel so much more different then I had ever felt before. It became a steroid to my body, my soul, my mind and my heart. I started to have some of the worst nightmares ever. Many times over I would see my reflection in a mirror but it was not me. My face had morphed into a demon's face. Long hair, long teeth and cat like eyes. In my dream I would be eating live animals and drinking their blood. My mom and I had a little dog when I was growing up and she would always sleep with me. It got to the point where I finally had to tell my mom what was going on because it was no longer safe for my little dog to sleep with me. I would wake up every night in a cold sweat, shaking from head to toe. The point that I finally understood I had hit rock bottom was one night when I was facing the wall, I heard the sound of heavy breathing at the end of my bed, then it began to make a dragging sound along the floor of my bedroom and came to a stop at the head of my bed. I could not stop crying, I felt so weak and lost. I told my mom everything I had been doing. I told her how I had begun to pray to satan and had literally invited him into my life and our home. Between what was going on at that moment and before when we began to hear footsteps throughout the house, it was not long after that, we moved. Through it all I can never put into words how bad I hated everyone and mainly God. It got so bad my body would literally shake in the presence of someone that was a Christian. I would cringe at the idea of being near a church. This is why I believe that Satan can and will appear as the most beautiful being you could ever imagine, that is how he sets the trap. For those of you that have never been through anything like this, let me tell you, you will never forget the feeling it leaves in you. When you stare into the darkness, it stares right back and consumes you from the inside out. The only way you can ever find freedom from that lifestyle is through the bloodshed of Jesus Christ. He can and will conquer all lifestyles. My heart had become stone and I had no compassion for anything or anyone. Jesus saved me. He showed me that he had never left my side. No matter what you have done, he is right by your side waiting.

Deuteronomy 18:9-12

"When you enter the land the LORD your God is giving you, do not learn to imitate the detestable ways of the nations there. Let no one be found among you who sacrifices their son or daughter in the fire, who practices divination or sorcery, interprets omens, engages in witchcraft, or casts spells, or who is a medium or spiritist or who consults the dead. Anyone who does these things is detestable to the LORD; because of these same detestable practices the LORD your God will drive out those nations before you."

Ephesians 6:11-12

"Put on the full armor of God, so that you can take your stand against the devil's schemes. For our struggle is not against flesh and blood, but against the rulers, against the authorities, against the powers of this dark world and against the spiritual forces of evil in the heavenly realms."

Jeremiah 10:2

"This is what the LORD says: 'Do not learn the ways of the nations or be terrified by signs in the heavens, though the nations are terrified by them."

Jeremiah 27:9-10

"So do not listen to your prophets, your diviners, your interpreters of dreams, your mediums or your sorcerers who tell you, 'You will not serve the king of Babylon.' They prophesy lies to you that will only serve to remove you far from your lands; I will banish you and you will perish."

DEMONS

M any people would like to believe that this next subject is nothing more than a lot of fairytales put together to scare us into living a certain way. The scary truth is that demons are more real than you could ever understand. They have many different names, but no matter what their names are, they're all the same. They're here to kill and destroy the human race. The truth about demons lies in the Bible. For thousands of years we have been hearing of all kinds of creatures and gods of the ocean or gods of the land. In the beginning of time when satan decided to start his own pointless following and took one third of all angels from heaven, a war against mankind started and from that point until now, they have tormented us in all kinds of different ways. Demons are shape shifters and they can deceive the most intellectual people known to man. They can haunt your dreams, your homes, and they can drive you to do things you would never think of doing. Everything from E.V.P., psychics, Ouija boards and other techniques of contacting the dead are nothing more than open doorways to demons. You are not contacting your loved one. Remember these demons are shape shifters and will imitate your loved one to the fullest just to get inside your head. The greatest trick that satan ever performed was convincing the world he didn't exist. I understand right now there are some who are saying well some of those psychics have solved crimes by contacting the victims. I'm here to tell you that it's not real. A demon is not above helping a human out to open a doorway to the rest of us. I'm sorry to say, there is nothing demons won't do just to get through to us. We have to be careful of what we watch, what we listen to or what we say. There are all kinds of doorways that can open and we have to make sure that we're not the ones throwing down the invitations because they will cross over. It's not a matter of if; it's just a matter of when!

Mark 5:1-13

"They went across the lake to the region of the Gerasenes. When Jesus got out of the boat, a man with an impure spirit came from the tombs to meet him. This man lived in the tombs, and no one could bind him anymore, not even with a chain. For he had often been chained hand and foot, but he tore the chains apart and broke the irons on his feet. No one was strong enough to subdue him. Night and day among the tombs and in the hills he would cry out and cut himself with stones. When he saw Jesus from a distance, he ran and fell on his knees in front of him. He shouted at the top of his voice, "What do you want with me, Jesus, Son of the Most High God? In God's name don't torture me!" For Jesus had said to him, "Come out of this man, you impure spirit!" Then Jesus asked him, "What is your name?" "My name is Legion," he replied, "for we are many." And he begged Jesus again and again not to send them out of the area. A large herd of pigs was feeding on the nearby hillside. The demons begged Jesus, "Send us among the pigs; allow us to go into them." He gave them permission, and the impure spirits came out and went into the pigs. The herd, about two thousand in number, rushed down the steep bank into the lake and were drowned."

James 2:18-19

"But someone will say, "You have faith; I have deeds." Show me your faith without deeds, and I will show you my faith by my deeds. You believe that there is one God. Good! Even the demons believe that—and shudder."

Matthew 12:24-28

"But when the Pharisees heard this, they said, "It is only by Beelzebul, the prince of demons, that this fellow drives out demons." Jesus knew their thoughts and said to them, "Every kingdom divided against itself will be ruined, and every city or household divided against itself will not stand. If Satan drives out Satan, he is divided against himself. How then can his kingdom stand? And if I drive out demons by Beelzebul, by whom do your people drive them out? So then, they will be your judges. But if it is by the Spirit of God that I drive out demons, then the kingdom of God has come upon you."

HELL

Most of the time when you talk about hell, you will hear people young and old mock it because no one can imagine God sending anyone to a place like that. The fact is, if the righteous can be rewarded for all the good that we do, then why can't the wicked be given what they deserve? Some people who do believe in hell don't believe in the flames or anything like that, they believe in it just being total darkness and a separation from God. I don't think that would bother anyone. I believe God knew he had to create something that strikes fear deep down inside of us. The way I see it is, sitting in total darkness is the same as telling Hitler he needs to go sit in the corner and think about what he has done. I believe his crimes against God's people justified the punishment against him. I've studied hell for a while now and have read up on all kinds of stories that are out there. Granted you can't believe everything you read or hear but I do believe in some of the stories that I've read. Some of the stories I've read on have talked about all kinds of things taking place in hell; everything from rape to dismemberment by demons. Some that have had near death experiences and have seen hell first hand speak about some of the most horrific things that you can only imagine.

People on fire, engulfed with maggots, and struggling to catch your next breath. Some say there are creatures down there that are so horrific looking and have such a stench of death about them that Hollywood at its best couldn't mimic them. I can't explain how real hell is. I do believe the only way to escape it is by receiving Jesus Christ as your savior. With that being said, I don't believe this should be looked upon as a scare tactic to convert you to Jesus. Accepting Jesus as your savior should be something you want to do for the sake of living a better life. Jesus doesn't send us to hell, we send ourselves. He told us how we can avoid going to hell. When we do the opposite of what he says to do, we are choosing to go there. People believe that it takes so much to get to heaven. I want to tell you that it takes less than you think to get to heaven. Jesus Christ is right by your side and waiting for you to let him in. He wants the best for you. You don't have to change a thing at all. You just have to say the sinner's prayer, give your whole heart to Jesus, and let him do the rest. If you have tried every other way and it's not working for you then why not try it this way? It's not my job to convince you, it's my job to tell you. What you do with it is up to you.

Revelation 20:14-15

"Then death and Hades were thrown into the lake of fire. The lake of fire is the second death. Anyone whose name was not found written in the book of life was thrown into the lake of fire."

Revelation 21:8

"But the cowardly, the unbelieving, the vile, the murderers, the sexually immoral, those who practice magic arts, the idolaters and all liars—they will be consigned to the fiery lake of burning sulfur. This is the second death."

Luke 16:22-24

"The time came when the beggar died and the angels carried him to Abraham's side. The rich man also died and was buried. In Hades, where he was in torment, he looked up and saw Abraham far away, with Lazarus by his side. So he called to him, 'Father Abraham, have pity on me and send Lazarus to dip the tip of his finger in water and cool my tongue, because I am in agony in this fire.'"

Matthew 5:22

"But I tell you that anyone who is angry with a brother or sister will be subject to judgment. Again, anyone who says to a brother or sister, 'Raca,' is answerable to the court. And anyone who says, 'You fool!' will be in danger of the fire of hell."

2 Peter 2:4

"For if God did not spare angels when they sinned, but sent them to hell, putting them in chains of darkness to be held for judgment"

DEATH

Generally when you talk about death, it's not an easy topic. A lot of people don't care to discuss it. I've come to realize the more I read the more I'm hearing people believing that death really is just the beginning. To be absent from the body is to be present with the Lord. I believe that when we pass on, Jesus is waiting with open arms. In 1993 my grandmother passed away from cancer but before she did, the last thing she told the doctor was, "I'm going home tomorrow." The doctor said that she was not going home because she was too sick. He had no idea what she was talking about. I believe Jesus sent an angel to welcome her home. The one thing you can count on is though it's not easy letting go of your loved one, you will be reunited. We are here for only a short time, so while we're here, we might as well make the best of it. Live for the moment and know that your life is a precious jewel in the eyes of God.

Romans 5:12

"Therefore, just as sin entered the world through one man, and death through sin, and in this way death came to all people, because all sinned—"

Ecclesiastes 7:2

"It is better to go to a house of mourning than to go to a house of feasting, for death is the destiny of everyone; the living should take this to heart."

2 Corinthians 5:8

"We are confident, I say, and would prefer to be away from the body and at home with the Lord."

Psalms 46:10

"He says, 'Be still, and know that I am God; I will be exalted among the nations, I will be exalted in the earth.'"

Ecclesiastes 7:1

"A good name is better than fine perfume, and the day of death better than the day of birth."

John 13:7

"Jesus replied, 'You do not realize now what I am doing, but later you will understand.'"

John 14:27

"Peace I leave with you; my peace I give you. I do not give to you as the world gives. Do not let your hearts be troubled and do not be afraid."

1 Corinthians 15:42-44

"So will it be with the resurrection of the dead. The body that is sown is perishable, it is raised imperishable; it is sown in dishonor, it is raised in glory; it is sown in weakness, it is raised in power; it is sown a natural body, it is raised a spiritual body. If there is a natural body, there is also a spiritual body."

HEAVEN

There are many different views of what heaven really is. Some believe that you just float around while others believe that heaven doesn't exist at all. I can't help but believe that after all that we have been through here on earth that we have a beautiful heavenly kingdom to go home to. Nope, unlike what some have thought heaven is not a place where all you do is float on a cloud and play a harp. There are many different accounts of people having near death experiences and going to heaven for a short time. Whenever they come back, they always have a hard time putting into words what they saw while they were there. They talk about the streets of gold, the reunions, the clothes, the music, the food or the angels. Some say they have had the pleasure of walking along the streets of gold with our Lord and savior, Jesus Christ. Heaven is truly home away from home. I pray that not only will I be there when my time is up but that I will see all my friends and family there as well. Don't miss out.

Genesis 14:19

"and he blessed Abram, saying, "Blessed be Abram by God Most High, Creator of heaven and earth."

Daniel 7:13

"In my vision at night I looked, and there before me was one like a son of man, coming with the clouds of heaven. He approached the Ancient of Days and was led into his presence"

Matthew 6:9

"This, then, is how you should pray: "'Our Father in heaven, hallowed be your name,"

Matthew 6:20

"But store up for yourselves treasures in heaven, where moths and vermin do not destroy, and where thieves do not break in and steal."

Matthew 19:23-24

"Then Jesus said to his disciples, 'Truly I tell you, it is hard for someone who is rich to enter the kingdom of heaven. Again I tell you, it is easier for a camel to go through the eye of a needle than for someone who is rich to enter the kingdom of God.'"

Luke 18:22

"When Jesus heard this, he said to him, 'You still lack one thing. Sell everything you have and give to the poor, and you will have treasure in heaven. Then come, follow me.'"

Revelation 21:1

"Then I saw "a new heaven and a new earth," for the first heaven and the first earth had passed away, and there was no longer any sea."

Revelation 21:10-21

"And he carried me away in the Spirit to a mountain great and high, and showed me the Holy City, Jerusalem, coming down out of heaven from God. It shone with the glory of God, and its brilliance was like that of a very precious jewel, like a jasper, clear as crystal. It had a great, high wall with twelve gates, and with twelve angels at the gates. On the gates were written the names of the twelve tribes of Israel. There were three gates on the east, three on the north, three on the south and three on the west. The wall of the city had twelve foundations, and on them were the names of the twelve apostles of the Lamb. The angel who talked with me had a measuring rod of gold to measure the city, its gates and its walls. The city was laid out like a square, as long as it was wide. He measured the city with the rod and found it to be 12,000 stadia in length, and as wide and high as it is long. The angel measured the wall using human measurement, and it was 144 cubits thick. The wall was made of jasper, and the city of pure gold, as pure as glass. The foundations of the city walls were decorated with every kind of precious stone. The first foundation was jasper, the second sapphire, the third agate, the fourth emerald, the fifth onyx, the sixth ruby, the seventh chrysolite, the eighth beryl, the ninth topaz, the tenth turquoise, the eleventh jacinth, and the twelfth amethyst. The twelve gates were twelve pearls, each gate made of a single pearl. The great street of the city was of gold, as pure as transparent glass."

MONEY

Some say that money is the root of all evil. There is nothing wrong with money itself. People bring a bad name to money. There are some people that do great things with the money they get; some help families in need, give to children, or help people off the street. Then you have some people who only care about themselves. You can't let money control you, you have to control the money. Money is not evil. God wants us all to prosper and be successful in our life. He wants us to have money and to enjoy it. He also wants us to live under his guidance and let him guide our lives so that we don't make too many mistakes. You should never be scared or ashamed to make money or have nice things. As long as you put Jesus Christ first in your life, everything should be fine.

Ecclesiastes 5:10

"Whoever loves money never has enough; whoever loves wealth is never satisfied with their income. This too is meaningless."

Isaiah 55:1

"Come, all you who are thirsty, come to the waters; and you who have no money, come, buy and eat! Come, buy wine and milk without money and without cost."

Matthew 6:24

"No one can serve two masters. Either you will hate the one and love the other, or you will be devoted to the one and despise the other. You cannot serve both God and money."

Luke 9:3

"He told them: "Take nothing for the journey—no staff, no bag, no bread, no money, no extra shirt."

1 Corinthians 16:2

"On the first day of every week, each one of you should set aside a sum of money in keeping with your income, saving it up, so that when I come no collections will have to be made."

1 Timothy 6:9-10

"Those who want to get rich fall into temptation and a trap and into many foolish and harmful desires that plunge people into ruin and destruction. For the love of money is a root of all kinds of evil. Some people, eager for money, have wandered from the faith and pierced themselves with many griefs."

2 Timothy 3:2

"People will be lovers of themselves, lovers of money, boastful, proud, abusive, disobedient to their parents, ungrateful, unholy,"

Hebrews 13:5

"Keep your lives free from the love of money and be content with what you have, because God has said, 'Never will I leave you; never will I forsake you.'"

CHARITY

Working with charities is something I am becoming more and more focused on in my life. To give from the heart is one of the greatest feelings in the world. Charities are something in life that we can come together as one and truly show the love of God, to the ones in need. There are many different charities that you can donate to. Everyone from all over the world needs help. It is important that we remember what Jesus Christ did for so many people when he walked the earth. From soldiers to prisoners, from children to the elderly and everyone in between, we need to unite in the name of Jesus and help these people. Let the love of the Messiah show through our actions.

Philippians 2:4-5

"not looking to your own interests but each of you to the interests of the others. In your relationships with one another, have the same mindset as Christ Jesus:"

Proverbs 18:16

"A gift opens the way and ushers the giver into the presence of the great."

Psalm 119:130

"The unfolding of your words gives light; it gives understanding to the simple."

Matthew 6:4

"so that your giving may be in secret. Then your Father, who sees what is done in secret, will reward you."

2 Corinthians 9:7

"Each of you should give what you have decided in your heart to give, not reluctantly or under compulsion, for God loves a cheerful giver."

Proverbs 28:27

"Those who give to the poor will lack nothing, but those who close their eyes to them receive many curses."

Matthew 10:42

"And if anyone gives even a cup of cold water to one of these little ones who is my disciple, truly I tell you, that person will certainly not lose their reward."

2 Corinthians 8:7

"But since you excel in everything—in faith, in speech, in knowledge, in complete earnestness and in the love we have kindled in you—see that you also excel in this grace of giving."

John 3:27

"To this John replied, "A person can receive only what is given them from heaven.""

GREED

G reed comes in all forms. It could be money, attention, food or anything else you can imagine. Sometimes it doesn't take much to draw you in. For a gambler, hitting the big one just is not good enough and they will push for more. Some people believe the more things you own and God sees you with, the better you look in his eyes. I have big news for some of you out there. God doesn't care about what or how much you have. You can't take it with you anyways. Years ago, it was believed that the American dream was being able to pay your bills, own your home, a car and a family. People screamed for cars, so we built them cars. Now they want flying cars. People screamed for homes, so we built them homes. Now they want million dollar mansions. Mankind screamed for freedom, so God backed off and gave them freedom. Now mankind is in unbearable debt, killing each other, hunger, diseases, drug addicts, and is on the road to a nuclear meltdown. Do you see where greed has gotten mankind? No matter what God has ever done for us, we have shown that it's not good enough. We always want more. We can't turn back the pages but we can change the future. Through the bloodshed of Jesus Christ we can be set free from the spirit of greed. Take time each day and give thanks to Jesus for all that he has done. Without him, life has no meaning.

Luke 12:15

"Then he said to them, 'Watch out! Be on your guard against all kinds of greed; life does not consist in an abundance of possessions.'"

Colossians 3:5

"Put to death, therefore, whatever belongs to your earthly nature: sexual immorality, impurity, lust, evil desires and greed, which is idolatry."

Proverbs 15:27

"The greedy bring ruin to their households, but the one who hates bribes will live."

1 Corinthians 6:10

"nor thieves nor the greedy nor drunkards nor slanderers nor swindlers will inherit the kingdom of God."

Ephesians 5:3

"But among you there must not be even a hint of sexual immorality, or of any kind of impurity, or of greed, because these are improper for God's holy people."

2 Peter 2:14

"With eyes full of adultery, they never stop sinning; they seduce the unstable; they are experts in greed–an accursed brood!"

DID JESUS CHRIST SIN?

Over the years there have been a lot of debates whether Jesus sinned or if he lived a pure life. In today's world, it's hard to think that someone could live a perfect life. Everyone else, I would agree with that. The thing we have to remember is that Jesus Christ is 100% man and he was 100% God. Some people believe Jesus and Mary Magdelen had a relationship. The biggest reason why this would not be possible at all is very simple. Jesus Christ was also 100% God when he walked the earth. It would have been no different from what happened with the fallen angels. Jesus was tempted in every way just like us but in no way, shape or form did he sin. If he had, God would have been a liar. God's character can not and will not be shaken.

Hebrews 4:15

"For we do not have a high priest who is unable to empathize with our weaknesses, but we have one who has been tempted in every way, just as we are—yet he did not sin."

James 1:13

"When tempted, no one should say, "God is tempting me." For God cannot be tempted by evil, nor does he tempt anyone;"

Hebrews 1:12

"You will roll them up like a robe; like a garment they will be changed. But you remain the same, and your years will never end."

Hebrews 13:8

"Jesus Christ is the same yesterday and today and forever."

1 John 3:4-5

"Everyone who sins breaks the law; in fact, sin is lawlessness. But you know that he appeared so that he might take away our sins. And in him is no sin."

1 Peter 2:22

"He committed no sin, and no deceit was found in his mouth."

2 Corinthians 5:21

"God made him who had no sin to be sin for us, so that in him we might become the righteousness of God."

Acts 3:14

"You disowned the Holy and Righteous One and asked that a murderer be released to you."

IS JESUS CHRIST THE ONLY WAY?

M ost people today believe that as long as you are a good person, you will go to heaven when you die. That simply is not true. You can do all the good deeds that you want to do but it doesn't mean anything if it's not being directed by God. Everyone has to understand that it's easy to talk about God, but only a few talk about Jesus Christ. Almost everyone on the earth believes in either God or some type of god. The name God has become just another word in our language. Along with that, so has the name Jesus Christ. Maybe even moreso. There have been so many different prophets that have claimed to be the Messiah but only one has proved it. No one else has healed more people than Jesus Christ. No one else has ever preached more love than Jesus Christ and no one else has ever died for our sins. Not to mention even if they did die, they were nevered raised from the grave. Jesus told us these things would happen. I believe not only that Jesus Christ is the son of God but I believe he is our savior. He is our only shot at true peace and true happiness. Don't just take my word for it, do your own research and read the Bible. Compare notes to other books and open your heart to the one true God, Jesus Christ.

John 14:6

"Jesus answered, "I am the way and the truth and the life. No one comes to the Father except through me.""

Acts 4:12

"Salvation is found in no one else, for there is no other name under heaven given to mankind by which we must be saved."

1 John 2:23

"No one who denies the Son has the Father; whoever acknowledges the Son has the Father also."

Romans 5:21

"so that, just as sin reigned in death, so also grace might reign through righteousness to bring eternal life through Jesus Christ our Lord."

1 John 5:11

"And this is the testimony: God has given us eternal life, and this life is in his Son."

1 John 2:2

"He is the atoning sacrifice for our sins, and not only for ours but also for the sins of the whole world."

Colossians 1:13-14

"For he has rescued us from the dominion of darkness and brought us into the kingdom of the Son he loves, in whom we have redemption, the forgiveness of sins."

John 17:3

"Now this is eternal life: that they know you, the only true God, and Jesus Christ, whom you have sent."

John 14:3-4

"And if I go and prepare a place for you, I will come back and take you to be with me that you also may be where I am. You know the way to the place where I am going."

John 8:51

"Very truly I tell you, whoever obeys my word will never see death."

IS JESUS REALLY COMING SOON?

Countless times I have talked to people about if we are the final generation or not. Most don't believe we are. I want to take the time to point out some reasons on why I believe that we are the final generation. The first one is the explosion of technology. From the beginning of time to about 1900 or so we never saw cars, planes, TVs, computers, or electricity. No one before the 1960s knew what Global Communications was. Now they are inserting microchips in animals and humans. The microchips are able to track everyone, all medical records, and financial transactions as well. Another reason, Israel taking center stage. In 1948 Israel was established as a nation. All the Jewish people were once scattered to the four corners of the world. When Israel came together, the Jewish people came home. In 1967 Israel got control of Jerusalem after the six day war. From 70 A.D. to 1967 Jerusalem was in the control of the gentiles. Another reason: The revived Roman Empire. To the ones that don't know, that would be the European Union. Though there are many out there that don't believe that, I will tell you some facts to back this up. For one thing following from World War Two to now you will see the progress they have made. In 1947, The Marshall Plan was announced.

In 1951, the Treaty of Paris creates the European coal and steel community. In 1957, the Treaty of Rome transforms E.C.S.C. into European Economic Community. In 1986, Single European Act. In 1992, Maastricht treaty transforms E.E.C. into E.U. The stage was set for the Euro dollar. It is Brussels intent to seize control of a world currency. The latest report is that there are seven countries that are in the beginning stages of dropping the US dollar; Saudi Arabia, South Korea, China, Venezuela, Sudan, Iran, and Russia. Not if but when this comes to pass, it will be a sad day for America. America has to fall before the European Union takes the spotlight. The only way I can see America falling is because of the dollar. When that happens, America will have no choice but to join the European Union. Another reason: weather changes. Super-storms are breaking out all the time now. Earthquakes are destroying cities more than they ever have before. Record snow fall in the south, floods covering miles of land, and the list goes on and on. One final reason: a complete social breakdown including everything from the rights of Christians slowly being taken away to accepting abortion as a means of population control. The Bible warned us that in the last days, the final generation would be more cold and malice than ever before. What is wrong is now right and what is right is now wrong. This is it. All the signs that Jesus has warned us about have come to pass. The next event on the prophetic clock is the rapture. Ladies and gentlemen, this is it. If you have never asked Jesus into your heart, then I encourage you to do so. We only have today, tomorrow is not guaranteed.

James 5:1

"Now listen, you rich people, weep and wail because of the misery that is coming on you."

John 14:1-4

"Do not let your hearts be troubled. You believe in God; believe also in me. My Father's house has many rooms; if that were not so, would I have told you that I am going there to prepare a place for you? And if I go and prepare a place for you, I will come back and take you to be with me that you also may be where I am. You know the way to the place where I am going."

Revelation 1:7

"'Look, he is coming with the clouds,' and 'every eye will see him, even those who pierced him'; and all peoples on earth 'will mourn because of him.' So shall it be! Amen."

1 Thessalonians 5:2

"for you know very well that the day of the Lord will come like a thief in the night."

Matthew 24:42

"Therefore keep watch, because you do not know on what day your Lord will come."

Matthew 24:27

"For as lightning that comes from the east is visible even in the west, so will be the coming of the Son of Man."

Matthew 23:39

"For I tell you, you will not see me again until you say, 'Blessed is he who comes in the name of the Lord.'"

FORGIVENESS

This is a subject that I think everyone should read carefully. I believe that when Jesus Christ told us about forgiveness, he wasn't just talking about small things. He was also talking about the big things as well. I feel that we should try with everything in us to forgive for whatever has happened to us. Whether someone has stolen money, attacked you, or yes even the ones who commit murder or child molestation. I can speak from experience and yes I have forgiven them who were involved but no, I don't understand why it happened. The first time it happened I was 5 years old in Kindergarten and it was another student not much older than me. The second time I was eight years old and it was also by an older boy that I played baseball with. Then when I was ten years old I was at a friend's house and his dad thought it would be funny to flash me as a joke. Life is too short to hang onto the past. Everyone deserves a second chance in life. We all have sin in our lives. I know it's not easy and I never said it would be, but I do believe that if you ask Jesus Christ to help you to forgive, he will. If you will turn to Jesus, he will do the rest.

Matthew 6:14-15

"For if you forgive other people when they sin against you, your heavenly Father will also forgive you. But if you do not forgive others their sins, your Father will not forgive your sins."

Colossians 3:13

"Bear with each other and forgive one another if any of you has a grievance against someone. Forgive as the Lord forgave you."

Ephesians 4:32

"Be kind and compassionate to one another, forgiving each other, just as in Christ God forgave you."

Psalm 130:4

"But with you there is forgiveness, so that we can, with reverence, serve you."

Nehemiah 9:17-18

"They refused to listen and failed to remember the miracles you performed among them. They became stiff-necked and in their rebellion appointed a leader in order to return to their slavery. But you are a forgiving God, gracious and compassionate, slow to anger and abounding in love. Therefore you did not desert them, even when they cast for themselves an image of a calf and said, 'This is your god, who brought you up out of Egypt,' or when they committed awful blasphemies."

Colossians 1:14

"in whom we have redemption, the forgiveness of sins."

COMPASSION

It seems to me that over the years one of the great things that have helped mankind continue on has been compassion. God created us that way. God illustrates his love through us. When we help each other it shows the true nature of who God really is. Life is too short and who are we to determine who receives compassion. God tells us in his word to forgive no matter what someone has done to us. No one is saying It's easy but with the power of Jesus Christ, you can do anything. Everyone needs a second chance in life. When you save one life, that one life could go on to save one hundred more lives and so on. You never know what may happen. The greatest way you can show compassion in the world today is to 'pay it forward'. You help out three people with the promise that they will then help out three other people. Then before you know it everyone's eyes will be opened to what true compassion is.

Psalms 103:13

"As a father has compassion on his children, so the LORD has compassion on those who fear him;"

Mark 8:2

"I have compassion for these people; they have already been with me three days and have nothing to eat."

Ephesians 4:32

"Be kind and compassionate to one another, forgiving each other, just as in Christ God forgave you."

James 5:11

"As you know, we count as blessed those who have persevered. You have heard of Job's perseverance and have seen what the Lord finally brought about. The Lord is full of compassion and mercy."

Isaiah 49:13

"Shout for joy, you heavens; rejoice, you earth; burst into song, you mountains! For the LORD comforts his people and will have compassion on his afflicted ones."

1 Peter 3:8

"Finally, all of you, be like-minded, be sympathetic, love one another, be compassionate and humble."

Nehemiah 9:28

"But as soon as they were at rest, they again did what was evil in your sight. Then you abandoned them to the hand of their enemies so that they ruled over them. And when they cried out to you again, you heard from heaven, and in your compassion you delivered them time after time."

LOVE

There are many different types of love in the world today. The love between wife and husband, parent and child, and then there is the 'agape' love. Agape love is the strongest love in the world. It's an unconditional love that stands the test of time. No matter what we do to Jesus Christ, he is still by our side. People have used the word love very loosely and no one takes it seriously anymore. Though it would be wonderful, man has a very hard time believing in agape love because with man comes imperfection. We love until something does not go our way or until someone hurts us. The beautiful thing about the highest level of love from God is that, no matter how we mess up or what we do to him, he will forgive us and keep on living us. He may not like how we live our lives at times but he truly loves us just the same. Open your heart to what Jesus can and will do for you.

Exodus 15:13

"In your unfailing love you will lead the people you have redeemed. In your strength you will guide them to your holy dwelling."

Exodus 20:6

"but showing love to a thousand generations of those who love me and keep my commandments."

Numbers 14:18

"'The LORD is slow to anger, abounding in love and forgiving sin and rebellion. Yet he does not leave the guilty unpunished; he punishes the children for the sin of the parents to the third and fourth generation.'"

Deuteronomy 6:5

"Love the LORD your God with all your heart and with all your soul and with all your strength."

Psalms 92:2-3

"proclaiming your love in the morning and your faithfulness at night, to the music of the ten-stringed lyre and the melody of the harp."

Psalms 100:5

"For the LORD is good and his love endures forever; his faithfulness continues through all generations."

Psalms 85:7

"Show us your unfailing love, LORD, and grant us your salvation."

Psalms 85:10

"Love and faithfulness meet together; righteousness and peace kiss each other."

Proverbs 10:12

"Hatred stirs up conflict, but love covers over all wrongs."

Proverbs 21:21

"Whoever pursues righteousness and love finds life, prosperity and honor."

ISRAEL

For thousands of years people have been fighting over Israel. Some will say that it belongs to the Palestinians and others will say that it belongs to the Jewish people. I believe that Israel belongs to the Jewish people and this is why. About 2100 BC (about 4100 years ago): Abraham was born with the name Abram in the Babylonian city of Ur (Iraq). Estimates as to the era in which Abraham lived can vary from 2100 to 1800 BC (sometime between 4100 years ago and 3800 years ago). God called Abraham to the land of Canaan (which later became Israel). God established a covenant with Abraham. That covenant, or promise, was passed down to Abraham's son, Isaac, and then Isaac's son, Jacob. Abraham's first born with his wife Sarah was named Isaac. Isaac was the father of Jacob, who was the father of the twelve tribes of Israel. Many people are aware of the Holocaust in which Nazi persecution led to the death of six million Jewish people. Jewish people have endured instense persecution for centuries before that. During the first and second centuries of this era, the Romans killed as many as 1.8 million Jewish people. And the ancient destruction of Israel by the Assyrians and Babylonians nearly destroyed the people and country of Israel. After the fall of the Babylonian

Empire, about 2500 years ago, many of the Jewish people that were in exile returned to their homeland. Perhaps no other group of people has endured as much persecution as have the people of Israel. All these countries that came after Israel in the past have fallen. America, the European Union and the rest of the world needs to understand this before it's too late. If you rise up against Israel, you will fall to her. This is God's country and these are his people. We need to stand by them. These are innocent people and if we are true to our word about freedom for tohers, then we will not put any pressure on them to give up their land. It is their home.

Genesis 15:15

"You, however, will go to your ancestors in peace and be buried at a good old age."

Hosea 3:4-5

"For the Israelites will live many days without king or prince, without sacrifice or sacred stones, without ephod or household gods. Afterward the Israelites will return and seek the LORD their God and David their king. They will come trembling to the LORD and to his blessings in the last days."

Romans 11:26

"and in this way all Israel will be saved. As it is written: "The deliverer will come from Zion; he will turn godlessness away from Jacob."

Genesis 15:18-21

"On that day the LORD made a covenant with Abram and said, 'To your descendants I give this land, from the Wadi of Egypt to the great river, the Euphrates—

the land of the Kenites, Kenizzites, Kadmonites, Hittites, Perizzites, Rephaites, 21 Amorites, Canaanites, Girgashites and Jebusites.'"

Jeremiah 31:10

"Hear the word of the LORD, you nations; proclaim it in distant coastlands: 'He who scattered Israel will gather them and will watch over his flock like a shepherd.'"

MUSLIMS

In today's world it has become very hard not to judge all by a few. I was raised to believe not all people are the same. I do believe that, though it can be difficult to see that at times. I believe many of the muslims in the world are good people. It's the extremists that are destroying the muslim people. I believe if we turn to Jesus and open our hearts to the truth, he will restore our hearts toward the rest of the world. We can unite with the Jewish people and the muslims under the power of our one true God, Jesus Christ. We're here for only a short time and in order for us to do that, we have to see and understand how precious life really is. We have to see lfie through the eyes of Jesus Christ.

John 13:34

"A new command I give you: Love one another. As I have loved you, so you must love one another."

Luke 6:27-28

"But to you who are listening I say: Love your enemies, do good to those who hate you, bless those who curse you, pray for those who mistreat you."

Romans 12:14

"Bless those who persecute you; bless and do not curse."

1 Corinthians 4:12

"We work hard with our own hands. When we are cursed, we bless; when we are persecuted, we endure it;"

Romans 12:17-21

"Do not repay anyone evil for evil. Be careful to do what is right in the eyes of everyone. If it is possible, as far as it depends on you, live at peace with everyone. Do not take revenge, my dear friends, but leave room for God's wrath, for it is written: 'It is mine to avenge; I will repay,' says the Lord. On the contrary: 'If your enemy is hungry, feed him; if he is thirsty, give him something to drink. In doing this, you will heap burning coals on his head.' Do not be overcome by evil, but overcome evil with good."

1 John 2:9-10

"Anyone who claims to be in the light but hates a brother or sister is still in the darkness. Anyone who loves their brother and sister lives in the light, and there is nothing in them to make them stumble."

WAR

As far back as we can remember, there have been wars. No one likes them, there not fun but when you choose to live in a world without Jesus Christ, it's only a matter of time. It's one of the most destructive things that can hurt a country. Countless lives are lost, the enemy is crushed and many more die by starvation or diseases. There's a lot of people around the world right now that feel we should not be at war. Well, I feel that we are doing the right thing after what happened after 9/11/01. My heart goes out to all the families out there that have lost someone. If not for the men and women over there right now you would not have the freedom to live the life you do and I would not be able to right this book telling you that. I do not oppose the idea of a one world government as long as it is under the right hand of Jesus Christ. We have tried it so many times before on our own and look how far that got us. We will never be at peace until we unite in Christ Jesus.

Psalms 27:1

"The LORD is my light and my salvation— whom shall I fear? The LORD is the stronghold of my life— of whom shall I be afraid?"

Psalms 144:1-2

"Praise be to the LORD my Rock, who trains my hands for war, my fingers for battle. He is my loving God and my fortress, my stronghold and my deliverer, my shield, in whom I take refuge, who subdues peoples under me."

Ecclesiastes 3:8

"a time to love and a time to hate, a time for war and a time for peace."

2 Samuel 22:35

"He trains my hands for battle; my arms can bend a bow of bronze."

Genesis 14:2

"these kings went to war against Bera king of Sodom, Birsha king of Gomorrah, Shinab king of Admah, Shemeber king of Zeboyim, and the king of Bela (that is, Zoar)."

Judges 18:11

"Then six hundred men of the Danites, armed for battle, set out from Zorah and Eshtaol."

Joel 3:9

"Proclaim this among the nations: Prepare for war! Rouse the warriors! Let all the fighting men draw near and attack."

Matthew 24:16

"then let those who are in Judea flee to the mountains."

BONDAGE

There are so many things in life that can impact our lives. From sex, drugs, alcohol, fighting and so on. Sometimes you just feel like you can't escape, like you are drowning in the sea of life or like life is a prison sentence. Shackle and chains holding us down and sucking the life right out of us. Jesus spoke many different times about breaking the cycle and living in freedom. God never wants anyone of his children to feel like life is just a prison sentence. God wants us to embrace life to the fullest and open our hearts to the freedom that we find in Jesus Christ. No matter what it is that you feel like is holding you back from living life to the fullest, turn to Jesus Christ. He's the only one that can and will bring you true freedom from within.

Ezra 9:9

"Though we are slaves, our God has not forsaken us in our bondage. He has shown us kindness in the sight of the kings of Persia: He has granted us new life to rebuild the house of our God and repair its ruins, and he has given us a wall of protection in Judah and Jerusalem."

Romans 6:20-21

"When you were slaves to sin, you were free from the control of righteousness. What benefit did you reap at that time from the things you are now ashamed of? Those things result in death!"

John 8:34

"Jesus replied, "Very truly I tell you, everyone who sins is a slave to sin.""

2 Peter 2:19

"They promise them freedom, while they themselves are slaves of depravity—for 'people are slaves to whatever has mastered them.'"

Romans 6:6-7

"For we know that our old self was crucified with him so that the body ruled by sin might be done away with, that we should no longer be slaves to sin— because anyone who has died has been set free from sin."

HUMILITY

There are so many things in life that can bring you to your knees. When I was seventeen, I had gotten it in my head that I was going to have an apartment with all kinds of nice things and that I really was not going to have to work all that much for it. I had a major shock to the system by the time I was eighteen. There was a point where I did not have any food and could not get anything so when it got to the point that I could not control it, I jumped in a dumpster. It was behind a Pizza Hut and when they threw out the leftovers, then that is when I moved in. I had not eaten in a couple of days and when you get to that level of hunger, you will do almost anything to get rid of it. Fast forward to eighteen months later, I was nineteen and living in a house that a friend and I were renting. The landlord had turned off the power and this was in the dead of winter. It got down to twenty two degrees that January and we had no food or anything. We had to sleep on the old hardwood floors in front of the fireplace. A lot of the windows where busted out and there was nothing keeping the cold from us. When you are lying on a hard splintery wooden floor, you begin to wonder just how you got to that point in your life. For me it was a wakeup call. You start to put everything in its right category. There were many times in my life that I have been brought to my knees. I believe it is important to go through life rather than around it. It is only by the grace of God that we find ourselves in all the craziness of the world.

Proverbs 11:2

"When pride comes, then comes disgrace, but with humility comes wisdom."

Philippians 2:3

"Do nothing out of selfish ambition or vain conceit. Rather, in humility value others above yourselves"

Proverbs 15:33

"Wisdom's instruction is to fear the LORD, and humility comes before honor."

1 Peter 5:5

"In the same way, you who are younger, submit yourselves to your elders. All of you, clothe yourselves with humility toward one another, because, 'God opposes the proud but shows favor to the humble.'"

Titus 3:2

"to slander no one, to be peaceable and considerate, and always to be gentle toward everyone."

PEACE

There are many different things in life that will bring you satisfaction but there is really only one thing in life that will bring you real peace. That is Jesus Christ. I'm not putting anyone down that has money or anyone that is working hard to get nice things in life. God wants us to have nice things in our lifetime and he wants us to prosper but he doesn't want us to become consumed with things. The only way you can truly turn from your past or from the weight of the world is through the bloodshed of Jesus Christ. When you ask him into your heart, it opens a whole new chapter in your life. You will find a peace that is beyond any understanding. Whatever is tearing your family apart or pulling you down and holding you back, Jesus can and will bring peace to you. He will be faithful and bring you out of it. Just open your heart and ask him.

Psalms 34:14

"Turn from evil and do good; seek peace and pursue it"

Psalms 85:10

"Love and faithfulness meet together; righteousness and peace kiss each other."

Romans 5:1

"Therefore, since we have been justified through faith, we have peace with God through our Lord Jesus Christ,"

Philippians 4:7

"And the peace of God, which transcends all understanding, will guard your hearts and your minds in Christ Jesus."

John 14:27

"Peace I leave with you; my peace I give you. I do not give to you as the world gives. Do not let your hearts be troubled and do not be afraid."

Isaiah 9:6

"For to us a child is born, to us a son is given, and the government will be on his shoulders. And he will be called Wonderful Counselor, Mighty God, Everlasting Father, Prince of Peace."

Colossians 3:15

"Let the peace of Christ rule in your hearts, since as members of one body you were called to peace. And be thankful."

PRIDE

There have been a lot of times in my own life when I have allowed pride to be present and I've had to learn the hard way. Sometimes when people are faced with a problem, they'll come up with every excuse in the world not to accept help. There was many times when I needed to talk to someone about my bills and I just couldn't bring myself to ask or accept any help. There is something though that is even scarier than that; knowing you need to help with your life and yet refusing to turn to Jesus for help. I understand because I was there at one point. Every second that passes by is a second that you can change it all around. There's no point in waiting any longer because you're not guaranteed the next day. Take all your problems to the feet of Jesus Christ and let him take it from there.

Proverbs 8:13

"To fear the LORD is to hate evil; I hate pride and arrogance, evil behavior and perverse speech."

Proverbs 16:18

"Pride goes before destruction, a haughty spirit before a fall."

Daniel 4:37

"Now I, Nebuchadnezzar, praise and exalt and glorify the King of heaven, because everything he does is right and all his ways are just. And those who walk in pride he is able to humble."

Romans 11:20

"Granted. But they were broken off because of unbelief, and you stand by faith. Do not be arrogant, but tremble."

SALVATION

In today's culture we have so many beliefs on how we get to heaven. Statistics show that there are about 2,000,000,000 christians on earth. I believe only about half are true christians. The reason why I believe that is because when they came up with that figure, they combined all religions. The Lord never walked on eggshells and neither should christians. The only way to heaven is through Jesus Christ! You have to accept that what he did at the cross was for you. You can't really take that first step with God until you confess to Jesus Christ that you are a sinner and that you need saving. Anything outside of the word of God is rejected by God himself. Words can never really make you understand what Jesus did for us. God allowed his son to be mocked, beat down, whipped, spit on, laughed at and thrown into prison. Think of how it would feel if you were God and someone did that to your child. Some may think that it's heartless to allow someone to do that to your child but imagine how much God loves us that he would come down in the form of man and suffer so greatly for us. Jesus does not care what lifeyou have or are currently living. If you will just say the sinner's prayer and turn your life over to Jesus Christ, you will be set free of whatever it is in your life. All it takes is that first step.

Romans 3:23

"for all have sinned and fall short of the glory of God,"

Romans 6:23

"For the wages of sin is death, but the gift of God is eternal life in Christ Jesus our Lord."

John 1:12

"Yet to all who did receive him, to those who believed in his name, he gave the right to become children of God—"

Revelation 3:20

"Here I am! I stand at the door and knock. If anyone hears my voice and opens the door, I will come in and eat with that person, and they with me."

1 John 5:11-13

"And this is the testimony: God has given us eternal life, and this life is in his Son. Whoever has the Son has life; whoever does not have the Son of God does not have life. I write these things to you who believe in the name of the Son of God so that you may know that you have eternal life."

1 John 1:9

"If we confess our sins, he is faithful and just and will forgive us our sins and purify us from all unrighteousness."

Ephesians 2:8-9

"For it is by grace you have been saved, through faith— and this is not from yourselves, it is the gift of God— not by works, so that no one can boast."

2 Corinthians 5:17

"Therefore, if anyone is in Christ, the new creation has come: The old has gone, the new is here!"

Romans 10:9-10

"If you declare with your mouth, "Jesus is Lord," and believe in your heart that God raised him from the dead, you will be saved. For it is with your heart that you believe and are justified, and it is with your mouth that you profess your faith and are saved."

John 3:16

"For God so loved the world that he gave his one and only Son, that whoever believes in him shall not perish but have eternal life."

CREATION

For many years there have been debates about how the world was made and where we came from. The world would have you believe that we came from monkeys, aliens and anything else to distract us from the truth. This all comes from satan. The greatest lie he pulled off was making the world believe he doesn't exist. Satan can't create, he can only destroy and he will go to great measures to deceive mankind. I've always had a hard time believing that the earth just happened to be in the right place at the right time. Not too far and freeze, not too close and burn up, meanwhile maintaining a perfect rotation. With all that can go wrong with this planet, I think we need to do a lot of soul-searching if we believe that it's all just dumb luck. We don't control anything and we never have. It's by the grace of Jesus Christ that this earth doesn't crush us. Through the good and the bad let's remember to give thanks to the creator and king of kings Jesus Christ.

Genesis 1:1

"In the beginning God created the heavens and the earth."

Genesis 1:26

"Then God said, 'Let us make mankind in our image, in our likeness, so that they may rule over the fish in the sea and the birds in the sky, over the livestock and all the wild animals, and over all the creatures that move along the ground.'"

Genesis 1:27

"So God created mankind in his own image, in the image of God he created them; male and female he created them."

Colossians 1:16

"For in him all things were created: things in heaven and on earth, visible and invisible, whether thrones or powers or rulers or authorities; all things have been created through him and for him."

Revelations 10:6

"And he swore by him who lives for ever and ever, who created the heavens and all that is in them, the earth and all that is in it, and the sea and all that is in it, and said, "There will be no more delay!"

Psalms 148:5

"Let them praise the name of the LORD, for at his command they were created,"

Isaiah 42:5

"This is what God the LORD says— the Creator of the heavens, who stretches them out, who spreads out the earth with all that springs from it, who gives breath to its people, and life to those who walk on it:"

1 Timothy 4:4

"For everything God created is good, and nothing is to be rejected if it is received with thanksgiving,"

ABORTION

I always wondered why someone would stand up and say 'no' to a puppy getting kicked around, someone fighting dogs, or even arguing the point about hunting; yet never say a word about killing a baby. For those of you who don't know what partial birth abortion is, well I'll explain it in a nutshell. It is where the doctor will remove all but the head and then he or shell will insert a tube like instrument and remove the brains out of the baby's head or snip the brain stem. I don't know how anyone could ever think of doing this to a baby. A lot of places have stopped this method of abortion but there are still places that don't care. Abortion is murder and it doesn't matter why you are getting it done, the baby is still suffering for what either you did or what was done to you. My heart goes out to someone that gets pregnant from a rape. I can't imagine how difficult that is but the baby did nothing wrong. Killing the baby will never take away what happened to you. You can always give the baby up for adoption. I don't believe for a minute that it is easy but it can be done. Jesus weeps when something happens to one of us. He loves us so much that he died for our sins. If this pertains to you, just ask him for help. Ask him to come into your heart and set you free.

Jeremiah 1:5

"Before I formed you in the womb I knew you, before you were born I set you apart; I appointed you as a prophet to the nations."

Luke 1:44

"As soon as the sound of your greeting reached my ears, the baby in my womb leaped for joy."

Psalms 22:10

"From birth I was cast on you; from my mother's womb you have been my God."

Psalms 139:13-16

"For you created my inmost being; you knit me together in my mother's womb. I praise you because I am fearfully and wonderfully made; your works are wonderful, I know that full well. My frame was not hidden from you when I was made in the secret place, when I was woven together in the depths of the earth. Your eyes saw my unformed body; all the days ordained for me were written in your book before one of them came to be."

Exodus 20:13

"You shall not murder."

Numbers 35:16

"If anyone strikes someone a fatal blow with an iron object, that person is a murderer; the murderer is to be put to death."

Romans 6:23

"For the wages of sin is death, but the gift of God is eternal life in Christ Jesus our Lord."

FAMILY

I can't express how important family is. When I was growing up I lived with my grandmother, mother and two aunts. It was a challenge for me as well as them. I was the only boy being raised by four women. I was very blessed to have the family that I did. When I was little I thought I would be a kid forever and I never thought about time. Now that I'm twenty eight years old I've learned that you don't live forever. I hear so many stories about how people had wished they had told their loved ones just how much they loved them or that they forgive them for whatever happened. My advice is stop putting off what you can tell someone now. Jesus never told us how long we have and the best way to honor him is to live every moment as if it was our last. Instead of hanging out in front of the television all day or playing video games, take the time to hang out with your children or mom and dad. Let them know you love them and want to spend time with them.

1 Timothy 3:4

"He must manage his own family well and see that his children obey him, and he must do so in a manner worthy of full respect."

1 Timothy 3:5

"(If anyone does not know how to manage his own family, how can he take care of God's church?)"

1 Timothy 5:4

"But if a widow has children or grandchildren, these should learn first of all to put their religion into practice by caring for their own family and so repaying their parents and grandparents, for this is pleasing to God."

1 Timothy 5:8

"Anyone who does not provide for their relatives, and especially for their own household, has denied the faith and is worse than an unbeliever."

FAMILY VALUES

A lot has changed over the years. When I was growing up it was mandatory that I showed respect to my mom and to my grandmother. I was taught to show respect to all elders. This new generation has no respect for anyone including themselves. On top of this problem, the public school system makes it even harder to bring our new generation up the right way. With them handing out condoms and telling children as long as they're safe, they can have sex, it's no wonder why this new generation has no self control. A few decades ago, it was them vs adults on how to live their lives. Now there's no one to tell them no. Everyone is saying go ahead and lvie the way you want and you don't have to answer for anything you do in life. This generation has a giant safety net under it. Not so much as helping our children but keeping them from answering for their mistakes. By not giving out condoms you're making them accept responsibility for their actions in life. If I tell someone not to rob a bank because of what might happen and they do it anyways, they bring judgement on themselves. The same applies to my children. I can tell them not to live a certain way but if they do then they have to answer for it just the same way I have. The only way we can get back to what we once had is to turn back to Jesus Christ. He is the truth, the light and the way.

Proverbs 15:27

"The greedy bring ruin to their households, but the one who hates bribes will live."

Proberbs 31:15

"She gets up while it is still night; she provides food for her family and portions for her female servants."

1 Timothy 3:4

"He must manage his own family well and see that his children obey him, and he must do so in a manner worthy of full respect."

1 Timothy 3:5

"(If anyone does not know how to manage his own family, how can he take care of God's church?)"

1 Timothy 5:4

"But if a widow has children or grandchildren, these should learn first of all to put their religion into practice by caring for their own family and so repaying their parents and grandparents, for this is pleasing to God."

1 Timothy 5:8

"Anyone who does not provide for their relatives, and especially for their own household, has denied the faith and is worse than an unbeliever."

WIFE/HUSBAND

Today I believe that more people are twisting the word of God to fit their lifestyle than ever before. When things start going bad in a relationship, you will hear people say 'well that's her job or that is his job because God says so." The truth is this generation wouldn't know what God's truth was if it bit them in the butt. Some men out there love to throw it around and do what they want because of what it says in the Bible. Here's the thing though, Jesus never said anything about running all over your wife. He never said you can treat her the way you want and have no regard for her heart. The Bible does say for women to be submissive to their husbands, not slaves. You cannot use that to win an argument or to get sex or anything else. That simply means for them to be our partners. I like to believe that marriage is a two part relationship, the velvet glove and the iron fist. The iron fist being working, taking care of all the problems, bills and so on. The velvet glove being the compassion and wisdom from a woman. It's not to say that men can't think from the heart but more often than not it's women that do. Now with that being said, to the women who belive you should be able to run over your husband and him stick around, bad news for you too. The man is to be the leader of the family. If the two of you are smart though, you will listen to each other instead of trying to override the other. Jesus wants the best for all of our relationships and he wants us to understand that we are a work in progress. Take the time each day to let your spouse know just how much you love them.

1 Corinthians 7:3

"The husband should fulfill his marital duty to his wife, and likewise the wife to her husband."

1 Corinthians 7:10-11

"To the married I give this command (not I, but the Lord): A wife must not separate from her husband. But if she does, she must remain unmarried or else be reconciled to her husband. And a husband must not divorce his wife."

1 Corinthians 7:13-14

"And if a woman has a husband who is not a believer and he is willing to live with her, she must not divorce him. For the unbelieving husband has been sanctified through his wife, and the unbelieving wife has been sanctified through her believing husband. Otherwise your children would be unclean, but as it is, they are holy."

1 Corinthians 7:39

"A woman is bound to her husband as long as he lives. But if her husband dies, she is free to marry anyone she wishes, but he must belong to the Lord."

1 Timothy 3:2-4

"Now the overseer is to be above reproach, faithful to his wife, temperate, self-controlled, respectable, hospitable, able to teach, not given to drunkenness, not violent but gentle, not quarrelsome, not a lover of money. He must manage his own family well and see that his children obey him, and he must do so in a manner worthy of full respect."

Ephesians 5:33

"However, each one of you also must love his wife as he loves himself, and the wife must respect her husband."

HOMOSEXUALITY

Homosexuality is one of the most controversial topics in today's society. Most believe that you are born that way; others believe it is a choice you make. I believe the Bible makes it clear. Why would God create something that he stands against? Chapter after chapter, verse after verse declares that God stands against it and he would not create someone who is homosexual. Science has even come forth and said that there are no genes in the human body that determines a person's sexuality. With that being said, I do believe that we should still treat homosexuals with respect. I don't agree with their lifestyle and I don't believe that God cares for it either. I do know that God loves everyone of us no matter what kind of lifestyle we choose to have. Through the bloodshed of Jesus Christ we all have an opportunity to change.

1 Corinthians 6:4

"Therefore, if you have disputes about such matters, do you ask for a ruling from those whose way of life is scorned in the church?"

Genesis 9:12-13

"And God said, "This is the sign of the covenant I am making between me and you and every living creature with you, a covenant for all generations to come: I have set my rainbow in the clouds, and it will be the sign of the covenant between me and the earth.""

Leviticus 18:22

"Do not have sexual relations with a man as one does with a woman; that is detestable."

Leviticus 20:13

"If a man has sexual relations with a man as one does with a woman, both of them have done what is detestable. They are to be put to death; their blood will be on their own heads."

Romans 1:26-27

"Because of this, God gave them over to shameful lusts. Even their women exchanged natural sexual relations for unnatural ones. In the same way the men also abandoned natural relations with women and were inflamed with lust for one another. Men committed shameful acts with other men, and received in themselves the due penalty for their error."

STRESS

In today's world, there are all kinds of things to stress or worry about. Trying to get in that university or to get that promotion. Perhaps you are a single mom or dad that is doing the best you can. For some if not all, it can seem like it is a life sentence. When I was about twenty six, I was diagnosed with high blood pressure. I was rushed to the emergency room by my wife after my blood pressure came back 209/136. It felt like my head was going to explode. The doctor told me after looking at the x-rays of my brain, that I was closer to having a stroke than I ever knew, perhaps only days. I was supposed to have another doctor's appointment just 6 days later, but the hospital told me I probably would not have made it. It is an amazing feeling to have in the pit of your stomach after hearing that. From that point until now, I've been trying to reprogram myself and live a healthier lifestyle. That is why it is so important for all of us to open our hearts and minds to Jesus Christ. Let him in and become free of what is holding you back in life. Don't let your life slip away over something that is temporary.

Proverbs 12:25

"Anxiety weighs down the heart, but a kind word cheers it up."

Psalm 34:4

"I sought the LORD, and he answered me; he delivered me from all my fears."

Philippians 4:6-7

"Do not be anxious about anything, but in every situation, by prayer and petition, with thanksgiving, present your requests to God. And the peace of God, which transcends all understanding, will guard your hearts and your minds in Christ Jesus."

1 Peter 5:6-7

"Humble yourselves, therefore, under God's mighty hand, that he may lift you up in due time. Cast all your anxiety on him because he cares for you."

Psalm 42:5

"Why, my soul, are you downcast? Why so disturbed within me? Put your hope in God, for I will yet praise him, my Savior and my God."

Philippians 4:19

"And my God will meet all your needs according to the riches of his glory in Christ Jesus."

Philippians 4:13

"I can do all this through him who gives me strength."

LAZINESS

There are lazy people in the world and then there was me. When I was fifteen, I wouldn't help anyone out and didn't care to even humor you about it. I let the kitchen get so nasty that we had mold all over the dishes, roaches throughout the house, and maggots all over the counter. It was to the point that when you walked through the living room, you could see the maggots in the carpet. We had three dozen bags of trash on our front porch and another dozen bags throughout the house. I never showered and wore sour smelling clothes that hadn't been washed in weeks. My clothes literally had the smell of mildew on them. Some that know me now, have a hard time believing me due to the fact that I am a little OCD about my cleaning these days. Whether it's a job, a car, a house, or whatever the case is, you cannot let yourself become lazy like that. If you want anything in life, you have to work for it.

Proverbs 10:4

"Lazy hands make for poverty, but diligent hands bring wealth."

Hebrews 6:12

"We do not want you to become lazy, but to imitate those who through faith and patience inherit what has been promised."

Luke 10:7

"Stay there, eating and drinking whatever they give you, for the worker deserves his wages. Do not move around from house to house."

1 Corinthians 3:13

"their work will be shown for what it is, because the Day will bring it to light. It will be revealed with fire, and the fire will test the quality of each person's work."

Exodus 23:12

"Six days do your work, but on the seventh day do not work, so that your ox and your donkey may rest, and so that the slave born in your household and the foreigner living among you may be refreshed."

Deuteronomy 5:14

"but the seventh day is a sabbath to the LORD your God. On it you shall not do any work, neither you, nor your son or daughter, nor your male or female servant, nor your ox, your donkey or any of your animals, nor any foreigner residing in your towns, so that your male and female servants may rest, as you do."

PROPHECY

There are many different points of views on this subject. Some feel that it's science fiction and others believe that it's the word of God, strong and true. If you ask about 10,000 people if they believe the world will end or not, about half or more will tell you no. The rest will be split between the Bible and global warming. So many people over the years have talked about their generation being the one to see the return of Christ. The Bible clearly states that the final generation would see the birth of Israel as a nation and soon after the revived Roman Empire. For the ones out there that don't know, it is believed that the new roman empire is known to us as the European Union. A lot of top leaders and bank investors are backing the European Union to begin a one world currency. The same generation that would see the rise of these two giants would also witness a huge falling away from the Word of God. A national poll was done. Back in the World War 2 era, 65% of the nation was following Christianity and now only about 15% of America is following Jesus Christ. If we made it another 50 years I believe Christianity would become history. This among other reasons are why I believe not only in the Word of God but also that this is the final generation.

1 Thessalonians 5:20

"Do not treat prophecies with contempt"

2 Peter 1:20-21

"Above all, you must understand that no prophecy of Scripture came about by the prophet's own interpretation of things. For prophecy never had its origin in the human will, but prophets, though human, spoke from God as they were carried along by the Holy Spirit."

Matthew 7:22-23

"Many will say to me on that day, 'Lord, Lord, did we not prophesy in your name and in your name drive out demons and in your name perform many miracles?' Then I will tell them plainly, 'I never knew you. Away from me, you evildoers!'"

Romans 12:6

"We have different gifts, according to the grace given to each of us. If your gift is prophesying, then prophesy in accordance with your faith;"

1 Corinthians 14:39

"Therefore, my brothers and sisters, be eager to prophesy, and do not forbid speaking in tongues."

1 Corinthians 13:8-10

"Love never fails. But where there are prophecies, they will cease; where there are tongues, they will be stilled; where there is knowledge, it will pass away. For we know in part and we prophesy in part, but when completeness comes, what is in part disappears."

Matthew 24:23-27

"At that time if anyone says to you, 'Look, here is the Messiah!' or, 'There he is!' do not believe it. For false messiahs and false prophets will appear and perform great signs and wonders to deceive, if possible, even the elect. See, I have told you ahead of time. "So if anyone tells you, 'There he is, out in the wilderness,' do not go out; or, 'Here he is, in the inner rooms,' do not believe it. For as lightning that comes from the east is visible even in the west, so will be the coming of the Son of Man."

ADULTERY

There are many different doorways that can be opened to adultery. It was Jesus that said if you lust after anyone then you have already committed adultery. Everything from a look, touch, thought or word spoken. Most believe that if you look and don't touch then you're alright but the truth is, one day a look won't be enough. A look will lead to a thought, a thought will lead to a word spoken and even a word spoken will in the end lead to a touch. Just one doorway left open can lead to the destruction of your home, your marriage, and ultimately the downfall of your relationship with God. This is why I believe family values have gone right out the window. People today go into relationships like they're revolving doors. As soon as it gets bad or they get bored, they jump into another situation and bring sin upon themselves. You cannot let yourself give in to temptation. Be strong in the Lord. Lean on Jesus Christ and he will bring you above all the temptation of the world.

Exodus 20:14

"You shall not commit adultery."

Matthew 5:27-28

"You have heard that it was said, 'You shall not commit adultery.' But I tell you that anyone who looks at a woman lustfully has already committed adultery with her in his heart."

Matthew 5:32

"But I tell you that anyone who divorces his wife, except for sexual immorality, makes her the victim of adultery, and anyone who marries a divorced woman commits adultery."

Proverbs 13:15

"Good judgment wins favor, but the way of the unfaithful leads to their destruction."

Hebrews 13:4

"Marriage should be honored by all, and the marriage bed kept pure, for God will judge the adulterer and all the sexually immoral."

ADVERSITY

I would like to look at adversity as if it were Vegas, the house always wins. There's a lot of different ways you could look at adversity. One way is "What doesn't kill you only makes you stronger". The other way you could look at it is you could just roll over and die. I know that sounds a bit weird but we have to pick up our own crosses and move on. I myself have had many moments where I didn't think I would make it through but God never let me deal with more than I could handle. When I was 18 I had no food and no way of getting my food so when it got to the point of no return, I went dumpster diving. When I was 19 a friend and I were practically homeless. We were living in a house with no electricity in the dead of winter and most of the windows were busted out. So for about six weeks we slept on old splintery floors in front of a fireplace. When your laying on a cold floor and have very little food, you begin to realize what's most important. You forget about all the things that you thought were once important. Looking back I realize that Jesus was right there with us. No matter how big the mountain, he will bring it down for you if you let him. Open your heart today and let Christ lift you above your problem.

1 Peter 4:12-13

"Dear friends, do not be surprised at the fiery ordeal that has come on you to test you, as though something strange were happening to you. But rejoice inasmuch as you participate in the sufferings of Christ, so that you may be overjoyed when his glory is revealed."

1 Corinthians 10:13

"No temptation has overtaken you except what is common to mankind. And God is faithful; he will not let you be tempted beyond what you can bear. But when you are tempted, he will also provide a way out so that you can endure it."

Psalm 73:23

"Yet I am always with you; you hold me by my right hand."

James 1:12

"Blessed is the one who perseveres under trial because, having stood the test, that person will receive the crown of life that the Lord has promised to those who love him."

1 Peter 5:8-9

"Be alert and of sober mind. Your enemy the devil prowls around like a roaring lion looking for someone to devour. Resist him, standing firm in the faith, because you know that the family of believers throughout the world is undergoing the same kind of sufferings."